AIRCRAFT

Navy Combat Aircraft and Pilots

Henry M. Holden

Enslow Publishers, Inc.

40 Industrial Road   PO Box 38
Box 398   Aldershot
Berkeley Heights, NJ 07922   Hants GU12 6BP
USA   UK

http://www.enslow.com

To my wife, Nancy, with love

Library of Congress Cataloging-in-Publication Data

Holden, Henry M.
    Navy combat aircraft and pilots / Henry M. Holden.
        p. cm. — (Aircraft)
    Includes bibliographical references and index.
    ISBN 0-7660-1716-8
      1. United States. Navy—Aviation—Juvenile literature. [1. United States.
Navy—Aviation. 2. Airplanes, Military. 3. Air pilots, Military.] I. Title.
II. Aircraft (Berkeley Heights, N.J.)
    VG93 .H65   2002
    359.9'4—dc21

                      2001001746

Printed in the United States of America

10 9 8 7 6 5 4 3 2 1

To Our Readers: We have done our best to make sure all Internet addresses in this book were active and appropriate when we went to press. However, the author and the publisher have no control over and assume no liability for the material available on those Internet sites or on other Web sites they may link to. Any comments or suggestions can be sent by e-mail to comments@enslow.com or to the address on the back cover.

Photo Credits: United States Navy

Cover Photo: United States Navy

Contents

CHAPTER 1

The Tomcat and Top Gun

It is January 15, 1989. Two U.S. Navy F-14 Tomcats are patrolling the air over the Gulf of Sidra, near Libya. They have just received a call from a Navy E-2C Hawkeye, an early warning radar aircraft. Two Libyan MiG-23 fighter jets are seventy-eight miles away. They are heading straight toward the aircraft carrier USS *John F. Kennedy*.

The Tomcats see the MiGs on their radar. They push the throttles forward and speed toward them. They are ready for a fight.

Each F-14 Tomcat carries a crew of two. The pilot sits up front. Behind him a radar intercept/weapons officer controls the radar and missiles.

"Sixty miles and closing," reports the Hawkeye radar operator.[1] The MiGs are getting too close to the carrier.

The Tomcats are moving fast now. They must stop the MiGs. Trails of white-hot flames pour from the tailpipes as the planes reach supersonic speeds. Their powerful computers transmit their air speed, altitude, and direction to the pilots and to the Hawkeye and the aircraft carrier.

The enemy fighters are still coming. The Tomcats are only thirty miles from the MiGs. The Tomcats' monitors allow the pilots and weapons officers to see their target from more than thirty miles away. That is far beyond what an unaided pilot can see.

One of the weapons officers is ready to shoot an AIM-9 Sidewinder missile and needs to know the enemy's altitude. He calls and asks the Hawkeye. "Say angels?" *Angels* is the term used for "one thousand feet of altitude."

"Angels five," replies the Hawkeye.

"No, the bogie." *Bogie* is a term used for "enemy aircraft."

"Angels nine," replies the Hawkeye. The MiGs are rolling in at 9,000 feet.

An F-14 fighter plane carries two crewmembers: a pilot in the front seat and a weapons officer in the back seat. An aircraft carrier, as seen in the water, is the structure from which a fighter plane can take off. The fighter can also land on the carrier after its mission.

"Thirteen miles—Fox One," calls the first Tomcat. *Fox One* means he has just fired a missile at one of the MiGs.

"He is jinking right," reports the excited Hawkeye radar operator.

The enemy plane has seen the missile launch. The Sidewinder will home in on the heat from the MiG's engine. The missile's exhaust forms a white chalk line across the sky. It is heading straight at the MiG. The MiG pilot makes wild right turns to try to escape it. It is too late. A red fireball appears in the sky. The missile explodes the enemy fighter.

The second Tomcat radios: "I have the second one in my sights. Fox One."

A U.S. Navy F-14 Tomcat releases a laser-guided bomb while in a dive.

"Five miles . . . four miles," reports the Hawkeye. Another red fireball appears in the sky. "Good hit," he calls as the second fighter blows up.[2]

In six minutes, the fight is over. The two Libyan fighters never had a chance. They had gone up against U.S. Navy Top Gun pilots.

Top Gun

In 1968, during the Vietnam War, the U.S. Navy discovered that its fighter pilots had great records. For every three enemy planes shot down, the U.S. Navy lost only one. The Navy decided to create a fighter pilot school where it would train its best fighter pilots to be even better. The Navy calls this school the Naval Strike and Air Warfare Center. The pilots call it Top Gun. Top Gun teaches air combat maneuvers and improves a pilot's self-confidence. By 1972, Top Gun pilots were shooting down thirteen enemy airplanes to every one they lost.[3]

About one percent of the Navy's pilots attend the five-week Top Gun school. To qualify for Top Gun school, a pilot must have at least five hundred flying hours and show high leadership skills. He must also complete at least one tour on an aircraft carrier. The instructor pilots are usually graduates of Top Gun. They teach for three years. They also act as the "enemy." The students will dogfight them with simulated missiles during their training.

Top Gun teaches pilots to overcome doubts about their skills and the aircraft. They are taught to react instantly to situations rather than to think about them. Fighter jets travel faster than the speed of sound, and the pilots do not always have time to think about what to do. Their reactions have to be automatic.

Top Gun pilots have about one hundred dogfights with their instructor pilots. Every move the airplanes make is recorded. Later the pilots look at a videotape of their flying. They analyze what they did and how they did it. They also learn why they did what they did. This way they will be able to improve their performance for the next flight.

The highlight of the five-week course is the Alpha Strike. This is a full-scale simulated battle between the instructors and the students. The students try to attack a land-based target. The instructors try to "shoot down" the attackers before they reach the target.

During the simulated dogfights, the instructor pilots try to take advantage of the students' weaknesses. The students learn that it takes teamwork to beat the enemy.

The F-14 Tomcat

The F-14 Tomcat is one of the airplanes that pilots at Top Gun fly. It is 62 feet 7 inches long. It has a wingspan of more than 64 feet. The Tomcat can fly at Mach 2.4, more than twice the speed of sound. It has one six-barrel 20-mm cannon in the nose and four to six missiles on its wings.[4] The F-14 can track up to twenty-four targets at once and shoot any of them down with one of its missiles.

An F-14 Tomcat leaves the aircraft carrier during Operation Allied Force. The F-14 can fly faster than twice the speed of sound.

The Tomcat has a head-up display (HUD). This is a transparent screen above the instrument panel, directly in the pilot's line of sight. It displays important information from the plane's computers. Some of this information is data from the altimeter, turn-and-bank indicator, and compass. Blue Angels pilot Lieutenant Doug Verissimo explained that during dogfights, because of the HUD, he never has to take his eyes away from what's happening outside.[5]

The Tomcat was used in 1999 during Operation Allied Force. This was an air operation against targets in the Federal Republic of Yugoslavia. The Tomcats provided cover for the heavy bombers of the U.S. Air Force.

EA-6B Prowler

During actual combat missions, the EA-6B Prowler flies ahead of the Tomcats. The Prowler protects the aircraft, ground troops, and ships by jamming enemy radar and communications.

The Prowler carries a crew of four: a pilot and three electronic countermeasure officers. Two sit side by side in the front and two sit in the back. The 60-foot-long Prowler is a twin-engine jet that can take off from an aircraft carrier or from land. It can fly as high as 40,000 feet at 651 miles per hour. It has a wingspan of 53 feet.

The Navy Command

The U.S. Navy is a branch of the armed forces of the United States. Its mission is to keep command of the seas.

To accomplish this, it uses many different aircraft and ships, including aircraft carriers.

Navy pilots fly jet fighter planes, such as the F-14 Tomcat, that carry bombs and missiles on their wings. They also fly helicopters, which carry troops and supplies and hunt for submarines. To protect its fleet of ships in the waters around the world, the Navy flies patrol aircraft. They use the E-2C Hawkeye to search for enemy airplanes and missiles. They also use the long-range P-3C Orion to search for enemy submarines. Read on to discover more about these high-tech aircraft and the pilots who fly them.

A U.S. Navy EA-6B Prowler flies over an oil rig in the Persian Gulf. The Prowler flies in front of the fighter jets and interferes with enemy radar and communications.

CHAPTER 2

Hunting Submarines

The crew of the P-3C Orion can feel the tension. Some of them have dull, throbbing headaches. They have been airborne for almost six hours. The cockpit smells of oil, fuel, and sweat. There is an unidentified submarine somewhere below, in the Strait of Gibraltar. The Strait of Gibraltar links the Mediterranean Sea and the North Atlantic Ocean on the southern coast of Spain. It is an important choke point—a narrow opening of water through which all ships must pass. If an enemy submarine can get through undetected, it could sink ships and block the seaway. The P-3's mission: to look for submarines. If they find an enemy submarine, they must destroy it.

The P-3C Orion hunts for enemy submarines.

The P-3C Orion is named for the constellation Orion. The stars in this constellation form the shape of a hunter with a bow and arrow. Hunting submarines is the main mission of the 135,000-pound P-3C Orion. This four-engine turboprop plane is over 116 feet long. Turboprop airplanes are propeller-driven but use jet-turbine engines. The powerful 4,600-horsepower engines turn four 13½-foot propellers on each engine. (By comparison, a car has 150 to 200 horsepower.) The wings of the Orion stretch nearly 100 feet. It flies about 470 miles per hour and can remain airborne for up to 14 hours.

The Crew of the P-3C

The P-3C Orion has a crew of ten to twelve. It has three pilots; one is a relief pilot for long missions. It has a tactical coordinator (TACCO) and one navigator/communications officer. It also has two flight engineers and two acoustic operators called Sensor 1 and Sensor 2. The radar operator is called Sensor 3. One in-flight technician is responsible for any in-flight mechanical or electrical repairs. One ordinanceman is responsible for loading sonobuoys. Sonobuoys are cylindrical devices that are fired into the water to search for submarines.

There are two kinds of sonobuoys: passive and active. Passive sonobuoys detect sounds generated by subs. Active sonobuoys send out a sonar ping to locate underwater objects.

Hunting for the Sub

There is added stress on the crew. The Orion is flying like a roller coaster gone wild. The aircraft pitches and rolls in the turbulence. The seat harnesses bite into the crew members' shoulders. Drinking coffee or juice is impossible.

Above the roar of the engines, there is a sharp metallic bang. *Wham!* It sounds like a sledgehammer against the airplane. A sonobuoy has just been fired from the plane's belly. The cabin fills with the acrid smell of gunpowder.

Once the sonobuoys reach the water, Sensors 1 and 2 will use the sounds detected by the passive sonobuoys to identify submarines. The sensor operator can tell what

A P-3C Orion patrol aircraft takes a close look at two submarines. The P-3C can drop a sonobuoy that lands in the water. Crewmembers on the Orion can identify the sounds from the submarines.

type of submarine it is by its acoustic signature. An acoustic signature is a recording of the engine sounds and other noises a submarine makes. It is like the submarine's electronic fingerprint.

The acoustic signatures of thousands of subs are stored in a top-secret computer database. A computer on the Orion searches this database for sounds that match those of the submarine below. When it finds a match, the crew will know the identity of this submarine.

The submarine crew knows the Orion is getting closer. They can hear the pinging of the active sonobuoys. If they need to, the crew of the Orion can drop underwater bombs, called depth charges, to destroy the submarine. The Orion carries other bombs in the bomb bay as well, and Harpoon missiles under the wings. The bombs and missiles can be used on enemy surface ships.

The sensor operators listen to the data with headsets and watch it on monitors. They pass the information to the TACCO. He will decide where and when to launch the next sonobuoy, and he will tell the pilot what course to fly for the next launch.

"It is a crew aircraft," said Lieutenant Todd Carlson, an aircraft commander. "We're a team. No one person is going to save the day. We live or die on the efforts of everybody."[1]

Finding the Sub

After hours of tracking the sub, darkness falls over the P-3C. "The adrenaline is pumping when you track an unknown sub," said Carlson. "Everybody is hyped up. We could be tracking an enemy submarine. There is a sense of urgency."[2]

Roller coaster rides can be fun, but not if you are on one for fourteen hours. The crew of the Orion is tired and hungry. They are also excited. They have identified the sound of the mysterious submarine. They also have its exact location. It is the USS *Buffalo*, a United States vessel. This was a training exercise. If it had been an enemy submarine, they would have had to destroy it. The P-3C crew can now go back to their base and get some rest.

≡ E-2C Hawkeye

The E-2C Hawkeye is another type of hunter aircraft. With a 24-foot Frisbee-like radar dome atop the plane, the Hawkeye is a flying radar station. It searches the skies around carriers and other ships. It can warn the ships about enemy missile attacks or inbound enemy fighters as far away as three hundred miles. Then it can help plan an attack before enemy planes come within range of the aircraft carrier.

An E-2C Hawkeye launches into the air. Notice the large radar dome that is used to search the skies surrounding aircraft carriers and other ships.

The Hawkeye's powerful radar dome antenna revolves six times a minute. The antennas inside are linked to the electronic systems onboard the aircraft. Each rotation fills the radar screen with new target information. The targets—all the airplanes in the area—glow like small green fireflies on the screen.

The dome also houses the antenna for the Identification Friend or Foe system. Radar operators can tell if an aircraft is friendly or the enemy. Every airplane has a special code it automatically transmits to the E-2C. The code shows up on the radar screen. The Hawkeye knows which airplanes are friendly by the codes it receives.

Driven by a pair of turboprop engines, the Hawkeye can stay airborne for about five hours. The plane is 57 feet, 6 inches long. It can take off from an airstrip on land or from an aircraft carrier, but it is designed to operate from an aircraft carrier. With a wingspan of about 80 feet, it helps that the wings fold back for storage on the carrier.

With all the information it has, the Hawkeye acts like a traffic cop in the sky. Its onboard computers can watch more than 250 targets at the same time.[3] The Hawkeye normally carries a crew of five: a pilot, copilot, combat information center officer, air control officer, and radar officer. They train at the Carrier Airborne Early Warning Weapons School called TOPDOME.

A Penguin missile roars off an SH-60B Seahawk helicopter toward a surface target.

SH-60B Seahawk

Traveling at up to 155 miles per hour, the SH-60B Seahawk helicopter can hunt submarines and surface ships. The chopper is a twin-engine helicopter used for antisubmarine warfare, search-and-rescue missions, cargo transport, and special operations.

When it hunts submarines, the SH-60B can drop sonobuoys and torpedoes. It may also have two 7.62-mm machine guns. The crew of three or four can fire Hellfire or Penguin missiles mounted on external brackets.

When the active Hawkeye and Seahawk crews are not flying, they are stationed at sea on aircraft carriers. Life on an aircraft carrier can be dangerous and exciting.

CHAPTER 3

Aircraft Carriers

U.S. Navy aircraft carriers are the largest warships afloat today. They have long flat decks that are like floating runways. The decks allow airplanes to take off and land on the ship.

The USS *Enterprise* is the longest carrier in the Navy fleet. It is 1,123 feet long, longer than the height of a 100-story building. It is about 17 stories high.

Aircraft carriers carry warplanes around the world. These planes show American military strength to any country that threatens the United States or its allies.

There are twelve aircraft carriers in the U.S. Navy. Nine of them use nuclear power, which means the ships' engines are run using atomic energy. Uranium fuel produces this energy. The other three carriers have engines that burn fuel oil.

Nuclear-powered carriers can stay at sea without refueling for about thirteen years. Normally, however, carriers will sail for six months. While they are at sea, they make frequent stops in foreign ports and at U.S. bases. They will get supplies and give the crew time ashore. Then they will return to their home port.

An aircraft carrier is like a small modern city. It may have as many as 6,000 men and women on board. Over 500 are officers.[1] Half the ship's company takes care of

The aircraft carrier USS *Kitty Hawk* is getting ready to get supplies from the U.S. Navy supply ship *Tippecanoe*, center. The Japanese destroyer *Haruna*, on the left, is part of a joint fleet excercise.

the ship. The other half—the air wing—takes care of the airplanes.

The superstructure on the right, or starboard, side of the flight deck is called the bridge. This is where all aircraft activity is supervised. The left side of the carrier is called the port side. The front of the ship is called the bow and the rear is called the stern.

The primary flight control, called Pri-Fly, is the control tower located in the bridge of the carrier. There, the air boss controls takeoffs, landings, and the movement of planes on the flight deck. Like an air traffic controller, he also keeps track of those aircraft in flight near the ship.

The Flight Deck

The flight deck is the area of the aircraft carrier where planes take off and land. It is a dangerous place for the sailors who handle the airplanes. There is danger from spinning propellers and from the suction of jet engine intakes. Jet exhausts can also blow a sailor off the flight deck. For this reason, the sides of the carrier are equipped with special safety nets. "You cannot become concerned with the danger," said one sailor. "Otherwise you cannot accomplish the job."[2]

The flight deck is very windy. Sailors wear goggles to keep dirt out of their eyes. A helmet with thick ear pads protects their hearing from the blasts of the jet engines. All sailors on the flight deck wear a float coat. This is an inflatable life jacket. The sailors wear color-coded jerseys to identify their jobs. Known throughout naval aviation

The flight deck of the USS *Nimitz* is a dangerous place to work. Here a sailor directs an E-2C Hawkeye onto one of the catapults during launch preparations.

as "grapes," the sailors in the purple jerseys fuel the airplanes. They are like the aircraft carrier's gas station attendants. Blue jerseys are the aircraft handlers. Yellow jerseys are the plane directors; they are like traffic cops. Green shirts are the catapult and arresting cable crew. They help launch and land the airplanes. White is worn by medical personnel and the landing signal officer (LSO). The LSO guides the pilot down to land the airplane.

The carrier is also a noisy place. Day and night, the sound of planes landing and the roar of jets taking off can be heard throughout most of the ship. A 30-ton F-14 Tomcat certainly is not quiet when it slams down on the deck as it lands.

Plane Launching and Landing

Carriers have two runways on the flight deck. One is straight and the other is angled. Because it has two runways, it can launch two aircraft at the same time. It launches the aircraft from any of four steam-powered catapults located on the flight deck. Catapults are like slingshots. The sailors in green jerseys attach hooks to the nose wheel and to runners on the catapult. The runners slide along tracks on the deck. Steam is used to shoot the runners forward at high speed. In two seconds, the plane is launched into the air at almost 165 miles per hour. Behind the catapults are jet blast deflectors. These keep the white-hot flames from the jet exhaust away from the sailors and the other airplanes on deck.

Flight deck crewmen are surrounded by catapult steam as they get an F/A-18 Hornet ready for launch.

The carrier flight deck is smaller than runways on land. A landing airplane has to be stopped before it runs off the other end of the flight deck. As the pilot is coming in for a landing, he or she lowers a hook from under the tail. The pilot uses this tailhook to try to catch one of four arresting cables stretched across the deck. Pilots call catching one of the cables a trap. If the pilot misses all four cables, or if a cable breaks, the landing is called a bolter. The pilot will fly off the deck and try again.

Landing on a carrier is called "a controlled crash."[3] That is because the airplane is traveling at over 150 miles per hour, and the arresting cables stop it in about three

An F-14 Tomcat hits the afterburner before launching. The jet blast deflector behind the plane keeps the hot flames away from crewmembers and other planes.

seconds. Remarkably, an aircraft carrier can land a plane every thirty-seven seconds.

Hangar Bay and Other Decks

The hangar bay is below the flight deck. To save space, the wings of some airplanes fold. About half of the eighty to one hundred airplanes on a carrier are stored in the hangar bay. The rest are parked in tight clusters on the flight deck. Four huge elevators carry airplanes between the hangar and the flight deck. Large steel doors can be closed to divide the hangar bay into zones. This will protect the airplanes from fire in other parts of the hangar bay.

Several more decks are below the hangar bay. They serve as living quarters for the crew. They also store bombs and missiles, about a million gallons of jet fuel, food, and supplies. There are more than three miles of passageways in these decks. They connect more than two thousand compartments, which contain sleeping quarters, galleys (kitchens), toilets, workshops, and storage areas. The engine room is below the last deck and contains the nuclear reactors.

There is little personal space for the crew aboard an aircraft carrier. Enlisted sailors sleep in bunk beds called

An F-14 Tomcat (left) launches from one catapult as four F/A-18 Hornets wait to launch from the aircraft carrier USS *Enterprise*.

racks stacked three high. There can be from twenty to one hundred sailors in an area.[4] Sailors have a curtain they can draw around their bunk to give them privacy. Entertainment consists of television, news, sports, and movies. There are also exercise rooms, barbershops, and game rooms. Sometimes the crew can play ball on the flight deck.

Officers sleep in staterooms. The rooms vary in size from eight-to-ten-person to three-person, two-person, and one-person staterooms. The junior officers normally share the more crowded rooms. Officers in the rank of

Inside the bridge, air traffic controllers watch their radar screens. They need to make sure the airplanes are safe distances apart.

lieutenant or lieutenant commander who have had multiple tours at sea will sleep in two-person rooms.[5]

The staterooms have two-high bunk beds and small fold-down desks for writing. Each officer has a safe for personal items and classified papers. Roommates will usually share a television and VCR, and they can plug into the ship's cable television channels.[6]

Pilot Training

Navy and Marine Corps aviators are trained to land on aircraft carriers. (The U.S. Marine Corps is part of the Navy). They are the only pilots in the military that do this. They must learn to land on an area a little bigger than a football field.

Pilots need constant practice to make good carrier landings. They will usually take off and land at least once a day. One pilot said, "Flying is like an addiction. Once you start, it is almost something you have to do every day."[7]

Pilots must have several hundred flying hours before they are allowed to make their first carrier landing.

"The most challenging part of the job is bringing the plane back on board," said Lieutenant Robert Rathert, an F-14 Tomcat pilot. "The F-14 is incredibly large and does not handle well at slow speeds. It takes complete concentration to be able to put fear aside and get the job done."[8]

One of the airplanes that lands on a carrier is the F/A-18 Hornet. This is the type of airplane flown by the Blue Angels.

CHAPTER 4

Flying with the Blue Angels

The Blue Angels are some of the Navy's best pilots. They serve as positive role models for young people. They encourage young men and women to join the Navy and Marine Corps. The six F/A-18 Hornets they fly perform aerobatics at air shows. Aerobatics are unusual flying maneuvers such as rolls, loops, dives, and inverted flying.

The F/A-18 Hornet is the Navy's latest single-seat fighter jet. It is 56 feet long and has a wingspan of 37 feet, 5 inches. It can fly at about 1,400 miles per hour, almost twice the speed of sound. This twin-engine fighter also has twin tails. It is both a fighter and an attack bomber.

As a combat aircraft, it carries air-to-air and air-to-ground missiles and bombs. It has one 20-mm six-barrel gun mounted in the nose. The Blue Angels' Hornets do not carry guns or missiles in air shows.

The F/A-18 Hornet

One of the Blue Angels' Hornets has two seats. The two-seater is used for training and for giving rides to special visitors.

Imagine you are in the backseat of the Hornet. It is an ejection seat. There is a harness around your shoulders, and there are straps on your thighs. There is also a lap strap and lower leg restraints. You are part of the airplane.

You are about to take off. The pilot has his feet on the brakes. He pushes the throttles forward. The Hornet's twin turbine jet engines let loose a deafening roar. He pushes the throttles into full afterburner range and releases the brakes. The afterburners dump raw fuel into the exhaust for extra thrust. The fuel explodes inside the exhaust pipe. The plane shoots forward like a rocket. White-hot flames shoot out the exhaust pipe. In less time than it takes to read this sentence, you are traveling at more than 300 miles per hour.

The pilot pulls back gently on the control stick. The stubby wings begin to lift the airplane from the gravitational pull of Earth. The nose of the 28-ton jet pitches straight up. You rocket into the sky. You feel a giant, invisible hand pushing you back against your seat. You are almost unable to move. Seconds later the Hornet levels off at 8,000 feet. The runway below looks as small as a paper clip.

Blue Angels pilots feel extreme forces of gravity on their bodies. The amount of pulling on the body is measured in units called gs. One g is the normal force of gravity at the earth's surface. If a person weighs 100 pounds, three gs makes the person feel as though there

A solo Blue Angels pilot lifts his plane about fifty feet off the ground. The white smoke surrounding the airplane is really water vapor in the atmosphere. Pilots in the plane feel very strong g-forces during their flights.

are 300 pounds holding him down. The Blue Angels can experience up to seven gs.[1]

Gravity tries to pull the blood in a pilot's head to his toes. "You sweat. Vision blurs. You get light-headed. You can lose consciousness," said one pilot. "To stay conscious, I have to grunt and strain. You have to tighten your muscles like you're getting ready to lift a five-hundred-pound weight."[2] The Blue Angels pilots train to fight the g-forces by lifting weights every day.

Pilot Selection and Training

The Blue Angels are special. They are handpicked. Blue Angels pilots serve two years with the squadron. There are approximately 15,000 active Navy and Marine Corps pilots. Each year only about three are invited to train and fly with the Blue Angels.[3]

Pilots are selected based on their flying ability. They must have a good personal and military appearance. Because they speak with crowds of people, they must have excellent communications skills.

The Blue Angels' routine sometimes looks dangerous, but it is not. That is because of the training they receive. Each pilot must complete 120 training flights during winter training. Then he is qualified to perform a public demonstration. The tight Blue Angels' formation takes hundreds of hours to develop. Teamwork and coordination are necessary for the high-speed, low-altitude flying. They practice teamwork and their maneuvers until they have them perfect.

Show Time

Normally the Blue Angels fly six F/A-18 Hornets at air shows. Four fly together in formation and two fly solo routines. The Blue Angels fly some very low and some very high maneuvers during air shows. The highest is the vertical roll, performed by one solo pilot. The pilot flies the Hornet straight up to 15,000 feet while turning the plane round and round. The other solo pilot performs the sneak pass. He flies as low as 50 feet at over 600 miles per hour. Most maneuvers are flown between 460 and 575 miles per hour.

"One exciting maneuver the Blue Angels perform is a wingover. Four jets fly together in the diamond formation," said Lieutenant Doug Verissimo. "It is led by the flight leader, known as the Boss. On the Boss' command, all four jets will roll together. This team is built on trust!"[4]

The chief of naval air training picks the Boss. The Boss must have spent 3,000 hours flying a jet. He must also have been in charge of a jet squadron.

The Blue Angels fly the diamond formation. The Boss leads the group in jet number 1. To his left is jet number 3. The canopy is just 36 inches below his wing. The number 2 jet is on his right side and the slot pilot is in the number 4 jet. The nose of his airplane is underneath the Boss' tailpipe.

This trust and training is obvious when watching Blue Angels perform their solo routines. During a show the solo pilots fly head-on, toward each other. Their combined speed is 1,000 miles per hour. At the last possible second, they turn away and pass within three feet of each other.

"We're out to show off the jet's high-performance characteristics," said Lieutenant Scott Beare. "Such flying skill amazes the air show crowds." However, Lieutenant Beare tells children, "This is not impossible for you to do. I'm doing it, and I'm nothing special."[5]

Fat Albert Airlines

The Blue Angels TC-130 Hercules, nicknamed Fat Albert, is big and round. This large cargo plane is used as a transport vehicle, an electronic surveillance airplane, and for search-and-rescue missions. It can also provide aerial refueling for helicopters.

The TC-130 carries all the maintenance support people and equipment to set up the air show. Each engine of the four-engine turboprop delivers about 4,300 horsepower. It flies at approximately 350 miles per hour and carries about 25,000 pounds of cargo.

An all-Marine Corps aircrew flies Fat Albert. There are eight crew members: three pilots, two flight engineers, a navigator, a flight mechanic, and a loadmaster.

Fat Albert even gets to put on a show. The crew sometimes demonstrates the jet-assisted takeoff at air shows. Eight solid-fuel rockets are attached to the sides of

The Blue Angels TC-130 Hercules takes off and fires its jet-assisted takeoff rockets. The Hercules carries the maintenance crew and equipment to the Blue Angels' air shows.

the aircraft. These rockets help the giant transport climb to an altitude of 1,500 feet in just fourteen seconds.[6] "The experience is like a six-minute roller coaster ride," said Captain Dwight Neeley, a TC-130 pilot.

Navy aircraft serve many roles today to protect our seas and lend military support to our allies around the world. The tables on the next three pages list the aircraft currently flown by the Navy to help it accomplish these tasks.

Current U.S. Navy Aircraft

Fighter Aircraft

F-14 Tomcat—A supersonic, twin-engine jet fighter designed to attack and destroy enemy aircraft and ground targets. It can track up to twenty-four targets at the same time.

F/A-18 Hornet—The Navy's latest single-seat fighter jet. It can fly at about 1,400 miles per hour, almost twice the speed of sound. It carries air-to-air and air-to-ground missiles and bombs.

F/A-18E/F Super Hornet—About four feet longer, it can fly farther and carry more missiles than the F/A-18.

Early Warning Aircraft

E-2C Hawkeye—A twin-engine turboprop with a powerful radar that can detect airplanes and missiles up to 300 miles away. It provides early warning of enemy missile attacks on ships and warns of enemy fighters.

E-6A/B Mercury—The Navy equivalent of the four-engine Boeing 707 jet. Its radar monitors the sky for enemy fighter planes and missiles. It will also tell Navy fighter planes where enemy fighters are.

Electronic Countermeasures Aircraft

EA-6B Prowler—A twin-engine jet that protects aircraft, ground troops, and ships by jamming enemy radar and communications.

F/A-18 Hornet

F/A-18E/F Super Hornet

Antisubmarine Aircraft

P-3C Orion/EP-3E Aries II—A four-engine turboprop that patrols the waters for submarines.

S-3B Viking—A twin-engine jet aircraft used to search for submarines and surface ships. It can refuel other airplanes in air or drop underwater bombs to destroy enemy submarines.

Cargo Aircraft

C-2A Greyhound—A twin-engine turboprop used for onboard delivery of personnel and supplies to an aircraft carrier.

C-9B Skytrain II—The Navy version of the twin-engine Douglas DC-9 jet, used for passengers and as a flying ambulance.

C-12 Huron—A small twin-engine turboprop aircraft used for carrying passengers and cargo between military bases.

C-40A Clipper—The Navy version of the Boeing 737 jet, used for passengers and cargo. It will eventually replace the C-9.

C-130 Hercules—A four-engine turboprop plane used as a transport, an electronic surveillance plane, and for search-and-rescue missions. It can also provide aerial refueling for helicopters and has been used as a gunship.

Trainers

T-34C Turbomentor—A single-engine turboprop used for basic pilot and navigator training.

T-39N Sabreliner—Used to train Naval flight officers in radar navigation and as radar operators.

T-44A Pegasus—Used to train Navy pilots to fly multi-engine, turboprop aircraft such as the P-3C and the C-130.

P-3C Orion

C-130 Hercules

T-45A Goshawk—A two-seat plane used to train Naval aviators for carrier landings.

Helicopters

CH-46 Sea Knight—A twin-engine transport helicopter used for both land- and sea-based operations. It can carry 25 passengers, or 15 people on stretchers with 2 medical attendants. It can carry 10,000 pounds of cargo.

MH-53E Sea Dragon—Transport helicopter for up to 55 troops. It can carry a 16-ton payload 50 miles, or a 10-ton payload 500 miles. It can also drop underwater bombs to destroy enemy ships and submarines.

SH-60 Seahawk—A twin-engine helicopter used for hunting submarines, search-and-rescue missions, cargo transport, and special operations. It can drop sonobuoys and torpedoes.

TH-57 Sea Ranger—A twin-engine helicopter used to train student Naval aviators.

Tilt-rotors

MV-22 Osprey—A twin-engine tilt-rotor aircraft that takes off and lands like a helicopter. Once airborne, its engines can be rotated to convert the aircraft to a turboprop airplane.

SH-60B Seahawk

MV-22 Osprey

Chapter Notes

Chapter 1. The Tomcat and Top Gun

1. Actual cockpit recording. *Tom Cat Territory*, Startrax video, 1997.

2. Ibid.

3. Ibid.

4. *Jane's Encyclopedia of Aviation* (New York: Portland House, 1989), p. 449.

5. Bud Walker, "Eating G's with the Blue Angels," *Boys' Life*, December 1997, p. 40.

Chapter 2. Hunting Submarines

1. Author interview with Lieutenant Todd Carlson, July 26, 2000.

2. Ibid.

3. *Jane's Encyclopedia of Aviation* (New York: Portland House, 1989), p. 443.

Chapter 3. Aircraft Carriers

1. Tom Clancy, *Carrier: A Guided Tour of an Aircraft Carrier* (New York: Berkeley, 2000), p. 86.

2. *Aircraft Carrier* (video), Debonair Production Company for WGBH/Boston in association with Nova, 1994.

3. Ibid.

4. Author correspondence with Lieutenant Commander Jeff Breslau, Public Affairs Officer, San Diego, Calif., February 8, 2001.

5. Ibid.

6. Clancy, p. 122.

7. *Aircraft Carrier*.

8. Ibid.

Chapter 4. Flying with the Blue Angels

1. Donald R. Nelson, "Put Yourself in the Blue Angels' Cockpit," *Puget Sound Business Journal*, August 8, 1996, p.10.

2. S. Stuckey, "Flying with the Blue Angels," *Boys' Life*, October 1991, p. 36.

3. Bud Walker, "Eating G's with the Blue Angels," *Boys' Life*, December 1997, p. 40.

4. Ibid.

5. U.S. News New Vision, *The Blue Angels 50th Anniversary Edition* (video), 1996.

6. The U.S. Navy, *Blue Angels*, <http://www.blueangels. navy.mil/> (February 20, 2001).

acoustic signature—The specific sound a submarine makes.

aerobatics—Unusual flying maneuvers such as rolls, loops, dives, and inverted flying.

afterburner—A device in the tailpipe of an engine for injecting fuel into the hot exhaust. Burning the fuel gives the vehicle extra thrust.

air-to-air missile—A missile shot from one airplane at another airplane in flight.

air-to-ground missile—A missile shot from an airplane toward a target on the ground.

altimeter—An instrument for measuring altitude.

arresting cable—One of the four steel cables stretched across the flight deck that bring a plane to a complete stop via the plane's tailhook.

bogie—An enemy aircraft.

bolter—An unsuccessful landing on an aircraft carrier deck.

bow—The front of the ship.

bridge—The area from which all aircraft activity is supervised.

catapults—Steam-powered devices that launch aircraft from an aircraft carrier.

depth charge—An underwater bomb that is used to destroy a submarine.

flight deck—The area of an aircraft carrier where aircraft land and take off.

g—A unit of measurement for acceleration. One g is equal to the force of gravity at Earth's surface.

hangar bay—The area of an aircraft carrier in which some of the planes are stored.

head-up display—(HUD), a transparent screen in an aircraft directly in the pilot's line of sight that displays important information from the plane's computers.

port—The left side of the ship.

Pri-Fly—Primary Flight Control, the control tower for the flight operations on an aircraft carrier.

sonobuoys—Devices that search for submarines. Using sonar, they search for targets under the ocean.

starboard—The right side of the ship.

stern—The rear of the ship.

supersonic—Faster than the speed of sound.

tailhook—A hook attached underneath the tail of a plane that catches the arresting wire during landing on an aircraft carrier.

trap—A successful landing on an aircraft carrier deck.

turboprop—A propeller-driven airplane that uses a jet-turbine engine.

Further Reading

Books

Chant, Christopher. *An Illustrated Data Guide to Modern Aircraft Carriers*. London: Tiger Books International, 1997.

Courtenay-Thompson, Fiona, ed. *The Visual Dictionary of Flight*. New York: Dorling Kindersley, Inc., 1992.

Editors of Time-Life Books. *Carrier Warfare*. Alexandria, Va.: Time-Life Books, 1992.

Gaines, Ann Graham. *The Navy in Action*. Berkeley Heights, N.J.: Enslow Publishers, Inc., 2001.

Parker, Steve. *Flight and Flying Machines*. New York: Dorling Kindersley, Inc., 1990.

Internet Addresses

International Women's Air and Space Museum, Inc. © 1996–2000. <http://www.iwasm.org/>.

Lundgren, Johan. *Airliners.net*. © 1996–2001. <http://www.airliners.net>.

National Aeronautics and Space Administration. *Off to a Flying Start*. "Introduction to Flight." December 27, 1999. <http://ltp.larc.nasa.gov/flyingstart/module1.html>.

Smithsonian National Air and Space Museum. © 2000. <http://www.nasm.edu>.

The U.S. Navy. *Blue Angels*. <http://www.blueangels.navy.mil>.

The United States Navy: Welcome Aboard. <http://www.navy.mil>.

Index